For Russ: always by my side on every great adventure—L. S. S.

To Cian: your inquisitive spirit keeps inspiring me—A. C.

2023 First US edition
Text copyright © 2023 by Leisa Stewart-Sharpe
Illustrations copyright © 2021 by Aaron Cushley

Published by Charlesbridge
9 Galen Street, Watertown, MA 02472
(617) 926-0329 · www.charlesbridge.com

First published in Great Britain in 2021 by Wren & Rook
Text copyright © Leisa Stewart-Sharpe, 2021
Illustration copyright © Aaron Cushley, 2021
The right of Leisa Stewart-Sharpe and Aaron Cushley to be identified as author
    and illustrator respectively of this work is asserted. All rights reserved.

Library of Congress Cataloging-in-Publication Data
Names: Stewart-Sharpe, Leisa, author. | Cushley, Aaron, illustrator.
Title: How does chocolate taste on Everest?: explore earth's most extreme places
    through sight, sound, smell, touch, and taste / Leisa Stewart-Sharpe; illustrated by
    Aaron Cushley.
Description: First US edition. | Watertown, MA: Charlesbridge, 2023. | Audience:
    Ages 6–9 | Audience: Grades 2–3 | Summary: "An adventure to experience all five
    senses at the world's most extreme locations."—Provided by publisher.
Identifiers: LCCN 2022032565 (print) | LCCN 2022032566 (ebook) |
    ISBN 9781623544195 (hardcover) | ISBN 9781632893833 (ebook)
Subjects: LCSH: Extreme environments—Juvenile literature. | Senses and sensation—
    Juvenile literature.
Classification: LCC GB58 .S74 2023 (print) | LCC GB58 (ebook) | DDC 573.8/7—
    dc23/eng20230105
LC record available at https://lccn.loc.gov/2022032565
LC ebook record available at https://lccn.loc.gov/2022032566

Printed in China
(hc) 10 9 8 7 6 5 4 3 2 1

Display type set in Northern Lights by Mats-Peter Forss / Worn Out Media
    and Sookie by Skyla Design
Text type set in Blauth by Sofia Mohr
Printed by 1010 Printing International Limited in Huizhou, Guangdong, China
Production supervision by Jennifer Most Delaney
Designed by Diane M. Earley

How Does CHOCOLATE Taste on EVEREST?

EXPLORE EARTH'S MOST EXTREME PLACES THROUGH
SIGHT, SOUND, SMELL, TOUCH, AND TASTE

Leisa Stewart-Sharpe • Illustrated by Aaron Cushley

ini Charlesbridge

NOTE TO READER

Don't get too comfortable.

This isn't a curl up in the armchair, snuggle under the covers sort of book. Not even close! You're off on the expedition of a lifetime to experience the world's most extreme places through touch, taste, sound, sight, and smell. Soon you'll **feel** what it's like to stand in the middle of the desert, and your throat will tighten as you **taste** the last drop of water as it drains from your flask. You'll **hear** the thump of waves pounding your boat and wonder if you'll ever **see** land again. And at the end of your journey, you'll almost faint from the overwhelming **smell** of your socks. This is the world as you've never experienced it before.

It's going to be wild.

THE CALL OF THE WILD

In the desert, the sand is singing as it's whipped by the wind. In the forest, the trees are groaning and creaking as their branches rub together. The wild is calling. And it's getting **LOUDER**. There are untamed corners of our planet . . . corners where only the fearless tread.

It's time to answer that call!

There's a reason you've been wearing your boots to bed. They're nicely broken in now (and you'll be halfway to Greenland before your mom spots the mud on your sheets). From running up and down the school steps over and over again, to that grueling week of flipping tractor tires through the woods, your physical training is complete.

ANIMAL SURVIVAL 101

See a wolf: Climb a tree.

See a grizzly bear: Move slowly away.

See a tiger: Make a lot of noise and wave your arms.

(Best option: Don't get close to any of these animals!)

You're heading to eleven of the most **EXTREME** locations on the planet—the hottest, darkest, deepest, coldest, most magical places the world has to offer. Plus you'll go to a twelfth bonus location, too! It's going to be beautiful, breathtaking, and very dangerous. Luckily this journal is jam-packed with survival tips and the meanings of tricky words in the back. You're going to need all the help you can get.

FOOD SURVIVAL 101

Strychnine seeds: DON'T EAT!
You might not last an hour.

Slimy green water: DON'T DRINK!
It's got all sorts of nasty things in it.

Golden poison frog: DON'T TOUCH!
It looks cute but holds enough poison to kill ten adults.

Some days will be hard. Your feet will hurt. The fire won't light. You might even find yourself . . .

LOST!

LOST SCIENTIST FINDS UNLIKELY SAVIOR

Scientist **Agustín Fuentes** was tracking the mysterious maroon leaf monkey through the Borneo rain forest when he got helplessly lost! The forest is home to leopards and venomous snakes, and as the undergrowth rustled behind him, Fuentes feared for his life. Was it a clouded leopard? A pygmy elephant? A feral pig?

Suddenly he caught a glimpse of red fur— an orangutan! She held out her hand and calmly led Fuentes back to camp.

But the hard days will be fast forgotten as you see the world and all its incredible wonders.

YOUR ADVENTURE AWAITS

You're off to join the ranks of the world's greatest adventurers, who fearlessly blazed their own path. They clambered past nature's obstacles—the roughest trails and highest summits. And they ventured past physical and cultural barriers, too, pushing the limits of what their bodies could do and also what the world would allow them to do. They're going to be your inspiration for the challenging months ahead.

But hang on a minute. . . .

WHY ON EARTH HAVEN'T YOU PACKED?

Whip out that packing list and get started.

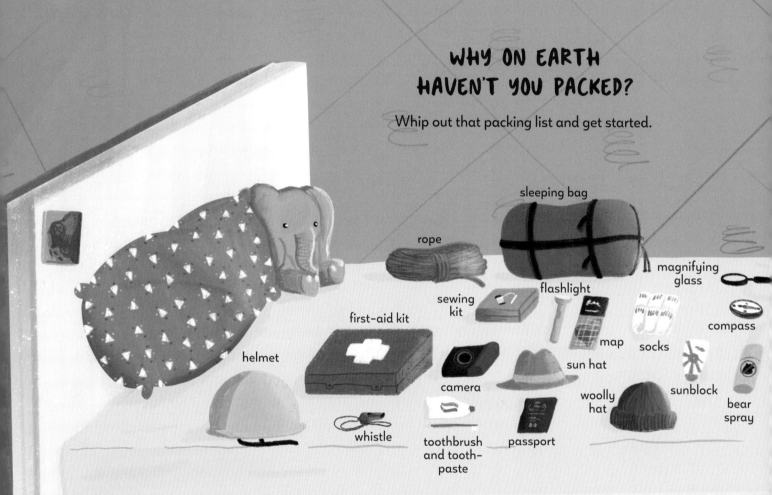

sleeping bag

rope

flashlight

magnifying glass

sewing kit

map

socks

compass

first-aid kit

sun hat

helmet

camera

woolly hat

sunblock

bear spray

whistle

toothbrush and tooth-paste

passport

PACK THE TOOTHBRUSH, LEAVE THE TEDDY

History's great explorers have differing ideas about what to pack on their travels. **Roald Amundsen** took a gramophone on his race to the South Pole. **Ed Stafford**, the first human known to walk the length of the Amazon River, says a machete is handy for putting up hammocks, chopping firewood, and descaling fish. Polar explorer **Ranulph Fiennes** isn't allowed to bring his toothbrush on expeditions because it's surplus weight. Your dentist wouldn't be too happy about that, so in yours goes.

Eric Larsen

First person to complete the Three Poles Challenge (North Pole, South Pole, and Mount Everest's summit) within a year (2010).

Philippe Croizon

First quadruple amputee to swim the English Channel (2010).

Valentina Tereshkova

First woman in space. She orbited Earth forty-eight times (1963).

You

backpack

Swiss Army knife

luggage tag

notebook and pencil

Your parents are expecting a postcard at every stop, so you'd better pack a pen, too.

boots

underwear

hammock

gloves

postcards and pen

THAT'S IT. YOU'RE PACKED!

But before you go, aren't you forgetting something? That's right—your water bottle. You won't last long at the first stop without it, because you're heading to the world's **HOTTEST** place! Your plane is waiting! *LET'S MOVE!*

THE DANAKIL DEPRESSION, ETHIOPIA

INSIDE THE BELLY OF A DRAGON

The plane's tires squeal as you touch down in Ethiopia in Africa. You'll spend the next five days exploring the Danakil Depression— a desert plain that's one of the hottest, driest, and lowest corners of the planet (where people can live). The hottest place on Earth changes from year to year, with Death Valley in the United States and Lut Desert in Iran fighting for the title, too.

It's going to be a sweaty drive to Dallol— the gateway to the Danakil Depression. You're traveling by jeep through the Afar region. Over millions of years, the area has been slowly sinking to more than 360 feet below sea level. Whenever the Red Sea floods the plain, the saltwater evaporates and leaves a thick layer of endless, silvery-white salt plains behind. The Afar people chop the salt, chisel it into bricks, and load it onto camels to sell at the local market.

As you get closer to Dallol, it feels like you're deep inside the belly of a dragon. Dallol's average temperature is 95 degrees Fahrenheit, but it has been known to soar to 120 degrees. The road soon becomes a dirt track—it's VERY bumpy.

BANG! Did you hear that? You've just blown a tire. Good thing you practiced changing tires on your dad's car. Grab the jack!

Hot air rises off the ground, shimmering mysteriously on the horizon. This is called a mirage. You can't help but wonder what secrets the Danakil might be hiding. After all, it was here in 1974 where paleoanthropologist **Donald Johanson** and archaeologist **Tom Gray** discovered the bones of 3.2-million-year-old **Lucy**. Lucy is one of our earliest ancestors, called an Australopithecus, and has taught us a lot about how humans evolved.

Back on the road, and a few spine-hammering hours later, your jeep skids to a stop. As the dust cloud settles, you step out into an alien world. The salt crust is fragile and cracking under your feet.

Watch your step. . . .

The world's hottest place:
THE DANAKIL DEPRESSION, ETHIOPIA

🔊 CAN YOU HEAR THAT?

This softly bubbling acid cauldron is Earth's lowest land volcano. As the water underground heats up, it collects chemicals—called minerals—from the rocks. The water pushes through the rock cracks and up toward Earth's surface. As it dries in the heat, beautiful colors are left behind from the minerals, creating rainbow hot springs in fluorescent yellows, reds, greens, and oranges.

👅 CAN YOU TASTE THAT?

If you thought the jeep was uncomfortable, then you definitely won't enjoy riding a dromedary (one-hump camel). It can drink fifty gallons of water in three minutes. You're so thirsty you try to match it gulp for gulp, guzzling water that got warm in the sun. Eww!

🐽 CAN YOU SMELL THAT?

After three days slowly plodding across the sand, your camel train crosses black lava fields. You get a whiff of something truly revolting. Don't blame the camels! It's the Danakil Depression's big, angry volcano: Erta Ale. It contains a large, active lava lake and smells like rotten eggs—that's from the sulfur coming out of the volcano. And the stench will only get worse as you start your three-hour climb to the top.

Sniff . . .

👁 CAN YOU SEE THAT?

Puffing and panting, you climb two thousand feet to the summit and peer into the volcano's mouth—a terrifying glimpse into Earth's boiling belly. Lava sloshes in hypnotic waves as Erta Ale hisses like a snake. But it's too hot, smelly, and close. You lurch backward as a giant lava bubble explodes near your shoes, and you gallop down the volcano. It's time for bed.

👆 CAN YOU FEEL THAT?

Ouch! You wake up, heart pounding, with an electric shock coursing up your leg. You've been stung by a scorpion! The same thing happened to British explorer **Wilfred Thesiger** when he was crossing the Danakil in the 1930s, even though his greatest fear was the hairy, plate-sized tarantulas that scuttled through camp. Let's hope you don't see one of those!

Your scorpion sting is a painful reminder of your time in Ethiopia. Cheer up! It's time to cool off in the Nile River.

Dear Mom & Dad,
I've sizzled through two pairs of shoes. Can you send my spare boots? I need to put my best foot forward!
XOXO

The world's longest river:
THE NILE

FROM SOURCE TO SEA

Your bottom is aching after bouncing across Ethiopia on a camel. But that's not the end of your bumpy journey. Next comes a week-long trip by jeep on rock-strewn roads, weaving through Kenya, Uganda, and Rwanda. That last country may hide something nineteenth-century explorers tried desperately to find—one of the starting points for the world's longest river: the Nile. The Nile has three main tributaries, including the White Nile, which some people believe starts in Rwanda. (Other people argue it begins in Burundi or the Democratic Republic of the Congo.) Your truck rolls to a stop—you'll go on foot from here, through the mountainous rain forest Nyungwe.

Watch your step on the slippery rope bridge!

In 1866, Scottish explorer **Dr. David Livingstone** set out to find the Nile's source. His supplies were stolen twice, he got very sick, and he was thought to be lost. In 1871, New York journalist **Henry Morton Stanley** went looking for him and eventually found him in a Tanzanian village.

Dr. Livingstone, I presume?

Livingstone believed the most distant starting point for the White Nile was beyond Lake Victoria, deep in the rain forest—something modern explorers also believe is true.

English explorer **Neil McGrigor** and New Zealanders **Cam McLeay** and **Garth MacIntyre** boated up the River Nile in 2006, using satellite technology to track the Nile's source.

You might expect the Nile to spring from the ground, but here in this muddy clearing, it's . . . trickling. The Nile ranges 4,100 miles through eleven countries on the way to the Mediterranean Sea: Tanzania, Uganda, DR Congo, Rwanda, Burundi, Ethiopia, Kenya, Eritrea, South Sudan, Sudan, and Egypt.

You trek for a week through thick forest, listening to the echoing chirrups of great blue turaco birds and the hoots of monkeys catapulting through the canopy. Finally the river becomes wide enough to launch your blow-up raft into its strong currents.

Are you ready?

The world's longest river:
THE NILE

👂 CAN YOU HEAR THAT?

There's grunting like a bullfrog on a megaphone.
If adventurer **Sarah Davis** were here, she'd say,
"GET OUT OF THE RIVER!" In 2019, Sarah became the
first woman to attempt to paddle the Nile River from source to
sea. But a few days in, a hippo chomped a hole in her raft when
Sarah accidentally came between a mother and her calf. That noise
is the sound of a very unhappy hippo. Best to give it a wide berth.

👆 CAN YOU FEEL THAT?

You've entered a stretch of rapids where the waves smash into
each other, spraying your face and sending your stomach
lurching. You grip the oars so tight that your fingers burn. You
paddle hard to go up, up, up and over the waves before being
tossed into the river. Your guide, Ntwali, hauls you back into the
raft. Gasping for breath, you suddenly realize the meaning
behind his name: "hero."

👁 CAN YOU SEE THAT?

Before the expedition, Ntwali placed a canoe behind some
bushes. You jump in, relieved to leave the wild water behind.
Peering through the papyrus reeds lining the banks of Lake
Victoria, you keep a close eye on the quiet crocodiles snaking
behind you. Green soon gives way to gold as you paddle
through the world's largest hot desert: the Sahara!

👅 CAN YOU TASTE THAT?

You don't want to become dinner for a sneaky croc, so you eagerly accept an invite for tea onshore. After you sit cross-legged on the floor, an enormous seniyya (platter) is placed in front of you. In Sudan you eat with your right hand, and you use flatbread to scoop up thick, spicy goat stew. Yum!

👃 CAN YOU SMELL THAT?

With a full belly, you step back into your canoe. In ancient times, clouds of sweet, woody-smelling smoke rose above Egyptian villages as people burned the spices frankincense and myrrh. But today the smell you've been waiting for drifts on the breeze . . . the sea! After seven months of paddling, you've finally reached the Mediterranean.

Time to journey toward the center of Earth. But first you must go up in this balloon!

Dear Mom & Dad,

I was laughed at by hippos and stalked by crocs, and I ate goat! I'm heading underground for some time away from the animal kingdom.

Wish me luck!

XOXO

The world's darkest place:
VORONYA CAVE, GEORGIA

JOURNEY INTO THE DARK

Are you ready to go spelunking? (That's the name for exploring a cave.) You're about to venture into one of the world's deepest and darkest caves: Voronya, also known as Krubera Cave. It starts high up in the mountains of Georgia (the country, not the state) and plunges down an incredible 7,200 feet at the deepest explored point. You could easily stack six Eiffel Towers inside. This mountain hides hundreds of caves, like a giant underground plumbing system. Voronya Cave is a complicated network of passages that wind almost ten miles underground. Don't get lost!

Your hot-air balloon sweeps over the mountains. When Russian priest **Fedor Konyukhov** flew his balloon around the world in 2016, he survived for eleven days with only half-hour naps. To keep himself awake and avoid crashing, he held a spoon between his fingers. If he dozed off, the spoon would clank onto the floor and wake him up!

Luckily your pilot's wide awake! She fires the burners, and as you gain extra height, you spot an open space in a valley carpeted in wildflowers. The pilot prepares to land. She releases the valve, and you crouch in the basket as it bumps and skids along the ground.

You're eager to start exploring the cave, but before you can go down, you've got to climb up 7,400 feet from sea level to its entrance. Spelunkers use some of the same gear as mountain climbers.

Two thousand yards of rope? CHECK!

Helmet? CHECK!

Oxygen tanks? CHECK!

Explosives?

EXPLOSIVES?

In some places in the cave, the passages are extremely tight. For many years, everyone who had been into Voronya said it was impassable beyond a few hundred yards. But Ukrainian speleologist **Alexander Klimchouk** said that there was no such thing as a dead end. His team spent years digging, and with the help of a few explosives, blasted through a boulder and unlocked what was, at the time, the world's deepest cave!

Voronya will be your home for the next couple of weeks.

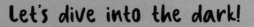

Let's dive into the dark!

The world's darkest place:
VORONYA CAVE, GEORGIA

CAN YOU HEAR THAT?

Voronya Cave means "Crows' Cave" in Russian. It got its name thanks to the crows that once nested in the mouth of the cave. You lower yourself down the remarkably small entrance and hear your helmet scrape on the rocks. Carabiners clink as they lock onto anchors in the rock face. The rope whizzes through your gloves, and you leave the light behind.

CAN YOU SEE THAT?

It's a maze down here. With only your headlamp beam, it's hard to know which tunnel to crawl through. You wonder what's scuttling in the dark. Perhaps it's the world's deepest land animal— the springtail. It has no eyes, but even if it did, what could it see in this eternal gloom?

CAN YOU FEEL THAT?

Waterspouts gush from the walls, leaving you drenched and cold, even in your dry suit. Creeping panic sets in as you shiver uncontrollably. Oh no, the passage is flooded! You bravely pull on your scuba gear and dive.

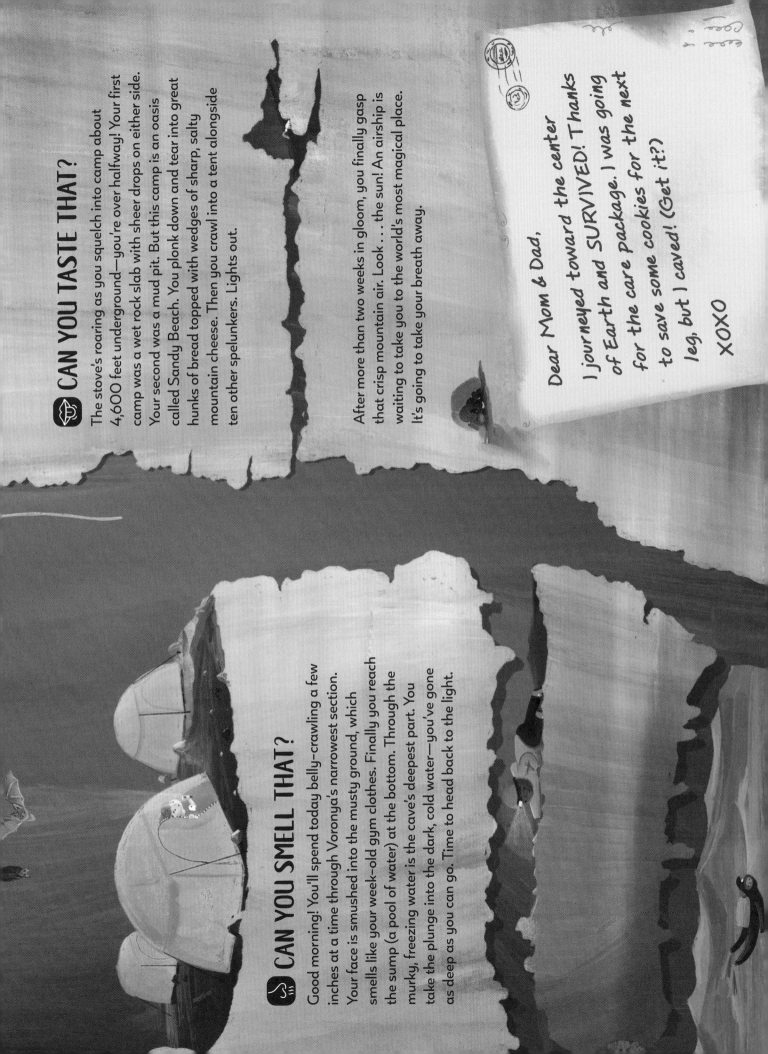

✈ CAN YOU TASTE THAT?

The stove's roaring as you squelch into camp about 4,600 feet underground—you're over halfway! Your first camp was a wet rock slab with sheer drops on either side. Your second was a mud pit. But this camp is an oasis called Sandy Beach. You plonk down and tear into great hunks of bread topped with wedges of sharp, salty mountain cheese. Then you crawl into a tent alongside ten other spelunkers. Lights out.

After more than two weeks in gloom, you finally gasp that crisp mountain air. Look . . . the sun! An airship is waiting to take you to the world's most magical place. It's going to take your breath away.

👃 CAN YOU SMELL THAT?

Good morning! You'll spend today belly-crawling a few inches at a time through Voronya's narrowest section. Your face is smushed into the musty ground, which smells like your week-old gym clothes. Finally you reach the sump (a pool of water) at the bottom. Through the murky, freezing water is the cave's deepest part. You take the plunge into the dark, cold water—you've gone as deep as you can go. Time to head back to the light.

Dear Mom & Dad,

I journeyed toward the center of Earth and SURVIVED! Thanks for the care package. I was going to save some cookies for the next leg, but I caved! (Get it?)

XOXO

The world's most magical place:
GREENLAND

DO YOU BELIEVE IN MAGIC?

What else would you expect from the North Pole? You board your airship—a balloon floating above a glass-bottomed gondola—and watch the world drift by below. You're the first person to ever take to the skies in this vehicle! Lighter than air, the ship is spirited away on the breeze. You're off to the world's biggest island: Greenland. You'll search for the magical Northern Lights, also called the Aurora Borealis. The best time to see it is in winter when the Arctic Circle is tilted away from the sun.

Robert Peary claimed to be the first to reach the North Pole in 1909. But **Matthew Henson**, his partner, stated that when the mist lifted, it was clear that his footprints were pressed into the snow first. The public at the time would never have accepted that an African American man could achieve this monumental feat. Meanwhile, rival explorer **Frederick A. Cook** said he reached the North Pole a year earlier. Claims of who was first are still disputed, but Henson's feats have at last been acknowledged.

AFRICAN AMERICAN EXPLORER MATTHEW HENSON FINALLY HONORED FOR INCREDIBLE POLAR ACHIEVEMENTS

Greenland rises above the horizon like a giant meringue with the ice whipped into peaks by the wind and waves. Below the ocean's dark depths, narwhals swim. Can they hear the polar bears padding above?

Brightly colored homes dot the shore. There are just over 56,000 people in all of Greenland, many of whom still live a nomadic way of life.

You've been practicing yoga positions for weeks to strengthen your stomach muscles in preparation for balancing on the back of a sled. As the airship dips, the gondola sways, caught by swirling wind currents. You tighten your seatbelt.

It's time to land.

The world's most magical place:
GREENLAND

Go!

🔊 CAN YOU HEAR THAT?

The airship touches down, and as the
engines are turned off, you're swallowed
up in a great snowy silence. That's soon shattered
by barking sled dogs. You take your position and shout
"Go!" The sled lurches forward. Your Inuit guide, Okila, runs
alongside the sled. His name means "fast runner." Now you know why!

👅 CAN YOU TASTE THAT?

You take a short break, and the dogs greedily chomp down their
lunch. As you watch them, your stomach grumbles with hunger.
Okila digs an ice hole with his tooq (ice pick) and catches a halibut.
You eat it raw, and its soft, sweet flesh melts in your mouth.

👆 CAN YOU FEEL THAT?

As temperatures plummet, you help Okila carve hard
snow, called pugaq, into ice blocks to form an igloo. This
will shelter you from the frosty air. When paralympian
Karen Darke made the epic journey across
Greenland on a sit-ski in 2006, the cold was
especially challenging. Karen is paralyzed
and can't feel anything from her chest
down, so she used a thermometer to
make sure her body never became
dangerously cold.

👃 CAN YOU SMELL THAT?

Tucked up inside your igloo, there's a faint smell of wet fur. At first you think it's the dogs. Then a looming shadow lurches past. A polar bear! Okila bangs cooking pots together, and you peek out to see the startled bear running away. In that moment, the clouds part and the starlit sky explodes in color. The Aurora has arrived!

👁 CAN YOU SEE THAT?

When tiny particles called solar winds stream out from the sun, they crash into Earth's atmosphere, letting off energy that paints the sky in swirling brushstrokes of pink, green, and blue. It's absolutely magical. You crane your neck to watch as the huskies howl at the sky.

In the morning, a plane skids onto the ice to pick you up. Next stop: the world's highest place!

Dear Mom & Dad,
I need a good bath.
Okila forgot to tell me that sled dogs poop while they run. Gross!
XOXO

The world's highest place:
MOUNT EVEREST, NEPAL

ALL ABOARD!

Your plane lands in Moscow. Now hurry! Once the Trans-Mongolian train leaves the station, it won't return for a week as it makes its mammoth journey across Russia, Mongolia, and China. Announcements drone overhead, and suitcase wheels rumble along the platform. You leap into the car and the train trundles forward. You speed past the wilds of Siberia, then through one of the world's biggest grasslands, the Mongolian-Manchurian Steppe.

Then you make your way to the Himalayas, home to the world's highest peak: Mount Everest. At 29,032 feet, it was first summited in 1953 by **Sir Edmund Hillary** and **Sherpa Tenzing Norgay**. More than six thousand people have since climbed Everest; **Kami Rita** has made the trek a record twenty-six times (as of 2022). But don't for one minute think it's easy. Climbing Everest is terribly dangerous, and about three hundred people have lost their lives attempting it. Almost thirty years before Hillary and Norgay climbed Everest, **George Mallory** and **Andrew Irvine** mysteriously vanished near the summit. Their camera may still be up there, holding the truth about their journey. Keep your eyes peeled!

But you're not going to climb Mount Everest. English adventurer **Holly Budge** skydived over it in 2008, free-falling to a nearby landing zone, and you want to follow in her footsteps. You're going to take in the mighty mountain from above—a view usually enjoyed only by the bar-headed goose. Your tiny plane bumps along the runway, and your teeth chatter as you take to the skies. You bank steeply right, and there, with its nose peeking through the clouds, is Everest.

The plane door is thrown open. Three, two, one . . . *JUMP!*

You plunge through the air, spinning like a yo-yo. The wind whooshes in your ears. Suddenly a huge gust sweeps you off course, and you *SLAM* into Everest!

Well, that wasn't supposed to happen . . .

The world's highest place:

MOUNT EVEREST, NEPAL

CAN YOU FEEL THAT?

You crawl out from under your parachute, not quite believing you've landed on Everest and survived! There's a crushing feeling in your chest, as though you're breathing through a straw. You're in Everest's death zone. There isn't much oxygen in the air at this height, so you need an oxygen tank to breathe well.

WATCH OUT for the big, hairy yaks. You don't want to get nudged over the edge!

CAN YOU HEAR THAT?

As night falls, you crawl into Camp Two. Sleep's impossible, thanks to the horrendous crash of rocks falling and the howling winds. Try not to think about what happened to Japanese mountaineer **Junko Tabei** and her team in 1975, when an avalanche roared down the mountain, blanketing everything in its path! Luckily everyone was pulled out alive. A few days later, a bruised and battered Junko continued her ascent and became the first woman to climb Everest.

CAN YOU TASTE THAT?

After hours grappling down the mountain, you stumble into Camp Four for lunch. The trouble is, the high altitude has made your appetite disappear. You need energy, so you tear open a chocolate bar and start to chew. Your heart sinks. It tastes like **NOTHING!** The altitude has dulled your taste buds, making every mouthful bland. You're going to need a stronger flavor. You reluctantly peel open a tin of slippery sardines and tuck in. Good protein, though!

👁 CAN YOU SEE THAT?

You've reached the scariest part of your descent: a giant glacier known as the Khumbu Icefall. In places the crevasses are so wide that three wobbly ladders are roped together to help you pass. Imagine what it was like for blind mountaineer **Erik Weihenmayer.** He crossed this very spot in 2001, becoming the first blind person to summit Everest.

Dear Mom & Dad,

I survived EVEREST!

I've spent the last few days celebrating with chocolate cookies, chocolate bars, and chocolate-covered raisins!

(Sorry about the smudges!)

XOXO

👃 CAN YOU SMELL THAT?

It's the smell you've been waiting for: wood smoke rising above Base Camp. You've made it! You survived Everest! No time to rest, because there's a cargo plane waiting to take you to the world's deepest place. Let's go!

The world's deepest place:
THE MARIANA TRENCH

GOING DOWN!

CLUNK! Your cargo plane drops its landing gear, ready to touch down on the Pacific island of Guam. Turquoise waters twinkle below as snorkelers glide over colorful reefs. But shallow waters aren't why you're here. The deep is calling. You board a giant expedition ship heading for the Mariana Trench in the western Pacific Ocean. The trench is a crescent-shaped crevice that stretches about fifteen hundred miles along the ocean floor—half the width of the United States. At 36,200 feet under the surface of the ocean, its lowest part, called Challenger Deep, could swallow Mount Everest whole.

Only a handful of people have ventured into Challenger Deep. **Don Walsh** and **Jacques Piccard** were first in 1960. Fifty-two years later, in 2012, filmmaker **James Cameron** zoomed down, too. It took him two hours and thirty-six minutes to reach the bottom. When **Victor Vescovo** made the journey in 2019, he saw plastic waste. Even the ocean's deepest corners aren't beyond pollution's reach. Most recently, former astronaut **Kathy Sullivan** made the trip in 2020 and became the first woman to do so.

Do you wonder which of the deep sea's mysterious creatures will swim by? The fish that lives deepest is the Mariana snailfish. It's fragile and transparent and appears to dance through the water. Other fish down there, such as the glowing hydromedusa jellyfish with its snakelike tentacles, light up the dark through a process called bioluminescence.

Your deep-sea submersible, called *Deepsea Challenger*, rests in its cradle. It's time to crawl through the hatch. Inside is smaller than a bathtub. Your knees won't unbend for the rest of the voyage. Remember all those days folded inside the training tank? You've got this.

SLAM! The hatch closes and you're almost ready to descend under the surface of the ocean. Your headset crackles:

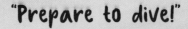

"Prepare to dive!"

The world's deepest place:
THE MARIANA TRENCH

👆 CAN YOU FEEL THAT?

Challenger Deep is a hadal trench—a deep crack in the ocean floor. It's bone-chillingly cold. Soon you're shivering from head to toe as your sub falls past steep cliff walls into the deep's inky embrace. Put on that sweater you brought! The pressure is a thousand times greater than at sea level. It's enough to crush every bone in your body. You're grateful to be inside your submersible! At 3,280 feet, all goes **DARK**.

🔊 CAN YOU HEAR THAT?

Suddenly an unexpected noise comes through the microphone. It's like a long, soft note from a cello.

Ooooheeeeehooooooh.

You're being serenaded by the world's deepest mammal: the beaked whale.

CAN YOU SMELL THAT?

It stinks like a damp basement in here. But it's still better than if you could smell underwater. Deep-sea fish have stronger scents than shallow-water fish because their bodies contain more of a special molecule called trimethylamine N-oxide. It stops them from getting crushed by ocean pressure, but makes them smell extra fishy!

CAN YOU SEE THAT?

After descending for two and a half hours, the submersible's control panel lights up because it's time to touch down. The seafloor stirs up as you gently land. Once it settles, you spot a strange carpet of microbial mats clinging onto rocks and transparent sea cucumbers inching along the seabed. It's out of this world.

CAN YOU TASTE THAT?

Uh-oh. Command says there's bad weather on the surface, so you're going to be stuck down here a little longer. The trouble is, you drank all your water! Time to dip into the emergency supply. It's ingenious, really. Your breath and sweat have collected on the metal sphere and been sucked into a plastic bag to drink. **CHEERS!**

Finally after seven hours underwater, you head upward, bubbles swirling all around. Good news: your solar panel is fully charged. Next stop: the Amazon!

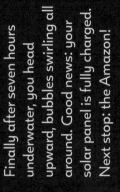

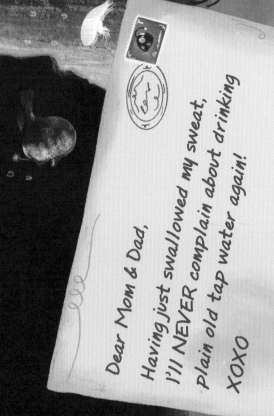

Dear Mom & Dad,

Having just swallowed my sweat, I'll NEVER complain about drinking plain old tap water again!

XOXO

The world's most secret place:
THE AMAZON

SSHHH! THIS NEXT PART IS A SECRET

You're flying over the Amazon, the world's biggest rain forest and even bigger secret keeper. There are vast areas of the Amazon that humans have never seen. It's sprouting, singing, crawling, climbing, flapping, and flowering with mysterious plant and animal species found nowhere else on the planet. Scientists discover a new species every other day! There are also more than seventy groups of people living there, and some have almost no contact with the outside world.

This huge rain forest is in nine countries: Brazil, Ecuador, Venezuela, Suriname, Peru, Colombia, Bolivia, Guyana, and French Guiana. Out the plane window, you glimpse a thick, lush canopy with the huge stripe of the Amazon River snaking through. The forest and river are enormous, and so is the wildlife! From lily pads big enough to stand on, to the twenty-foot-long green anaconda, about the length of a school bus!

It's easy to lose your way in this thick ancient forest. In 1971, seventeen-year-old **Juliane Koepcke** was flying over the Peruvian Amazon when her plane crashed, leaving her the only survivor. Unbelievably, she survived alone for eleven days, eating only a bag of sweets she found at the crash site before being discovered by forestry workers who took her to their village and found help.

GOLDEN SURVIVAL RULES

1. Don't eat unfamiliar fruit. It could be poisonous.
2. Don't worry about big animals. Insects rule here. Botflies lay eggs that hatch under your skin. Seriously revolting!
3. Find a river. Flowing water will lead you to civilization.

Your plane drops lower until you bump along a bush track. You'll spend the next few days trekking through the rain forest.

Now, where's that machete?

The world's most secret place:
THE AMAZON

👁 CAN YOU SEE THAT?

Light pierces the canopy as you stumble around giant buttress roots supporting the towering trees. Among the green leaves there are splashes of color. The blue morpho butterfly, one of the world's largest, appears then disappears, the brown underside of its wings camouflaging against the foliage.

✋ CAN YOU FEEL THAT?

It's like a heavy, wet blanket has been thrown on top of you. Billions of leaves release water, creating a thick cloud over the rain forest. It feels like honey has been poured into the creases of your neck and the bends in your elbows. You wish it would rain— anything to cool things down. Be careful what you wish for. . . .

〰 CAN YOU HEAR THAT?

The forest at night is eerily quiet, besides the low drone of insects and frogs. But then Mother Nature turns the rain on. It starts with a **TAP, TAP, TAP** high up on the canopy. Before long there's the thunderous sound of a million raindrops lashing the leaves and drenching you down to your undies.

👃 CAN YOU SMELL THAT?

Rise and shine! The screeching sound of singing cicadas wakes you from your slumber, and you take your first deep breath of the day. Ah, earthy soil, damp wood, and the unpleasant tang of mosquito repellent. You covered yourself head to toe, but there are still eighty-two mosquito bites just on your arm. When explorer **Ed Stafford** walked the Amazon River in 2008, his mosquito bites totaled a whopping fifty thousand!

👅 CAN YOU TASTE THAT?

Your belly's growling like a jaguar as you finally reach the river. Time to catch some breakfast. You cast your fishing line into the water. Soon there's a tug. . . . It's a bite! You haul in a fearsome piranha with razor-sharp teeth and roast it over the fire, hoping the smoke covers the strong fishy flavor!

Grab your canoe so you can paddle out of the forest. There'll be no time to dry out your socks, since a bus is waiting to take you to Venezuela. You've not seen the last of the rain.

Dear Mom & Dad,

I ate a piranha!

Half fish, half nightmare.
It tasted weirdly "muddy." I'll never complain about your cooking again.

XOXO

The world's most electric place:
LAKE MARACAIBO, VENEZUELA

THERE'S A STORM BREWING

If you thought the rain in the Amazon was bad, how about spending the night in an everlasting storm? But first these everlasting bus rides. You need to catch five buses to get you to the most electric place on earth: Lake Maracaibo in Venezuela, which is actually a tidal bay. You roll through Brazilian villages, over bridges, and through the passport checkpoint before finally crossing the border into Venezuela. As you stare out the window, your heart thuds with excitement. Table-top mountains, called tepuis, seemingly float above the clouds.

Lightning! AGAIN! What a shock!

After four days you finally arrive at Lake Maracaibo, South America's biggest body of water. The shoreline is dotted with brightly colored stilt houses called palafitos. You'll stay in one of those tonight when huge thunderclouds unleash the world's most frequent and intense storms, full of Catatumbo lightning, which is named for the nearby Catatumbo River. It lasts around ten hours every night about 297 days a year. (Catatumbo means "House of Thunder" in the language of the local Bari people.)

It won't be long until dusk, so get a move on! A local fisherman gives you a lift across the lake. His motorboat **PUTT-PUTT-PUTTS** as you weave between watery villages where laundry hangs between houses. You listen to the cries of howler monkeys over the rustling of palm fronds.

As you pull up, the air changes. Huge cumulonimbus clouds gather on the horizon as bats swarm against an amber sky. There's a distant rumbling like the stampede of a hundred angry elephants.

The storm is coming.

The world's most electric place:
LAKE MARACAIBO, VENEZUELA

👆 CAN YOU FEEL THAT?

Night falls quickly this close to the Equator, and the day's sweltering heat is broken at last. With no light pollution or crowded forest canopy, you enjoy the best view of the stars in weeks. The breeze starts to pick up and tickles your neck as you climb into your hammock and gently rock to sleep.

👂 CAN YOU HEAR THAT?

CRACK! You're blasted awake by thunder. The rain is pelting your palafito's tin roof—**RAT, TAT, TAT.** In the clouds water droplets turn into ice crystals and hail. As they bump into each other, they create an electrical charge: lightning. As it streaks toward the ground, it creates a shock wave and deafening thunder!

👃 CAN YOU SMELL THAT?

It smells like a swimming pool. That's the scent of the gas produced when lightning tears through the air. That other thing you can smell is fear, because that last lightning strike split a tree in half!

👁 CAN YOU SEE THAT?

The storm is all around you, and the sky explodes with lightning flashes—about twenty-eight per minute. Bolt after bolt reaches down like a witch's twisted fingers. It's so bright you could read a book in the dead of night. Storm chaser **George Kourounis** used the term *flang*: a flash-bang when the lightning and thunder are on top of each other.

👅 CAN YOU TASTE THAT?

The night is over. The storm has ended. The fisherman has returned. Better still, he's got breakfast: a basket of freshly baked arepas, and they are stuffed with scrambled eggs! You pounce on them like a hungry wolf, relieved to be alive.

The fisherman knows someone on a yacht bound for Australia. Guess what? They're looking for crew! That's an offer too good to refuse. Adios!

Dear Mom & Dad,
I should have packed
THUNDER-wear for Lake
Maracaibo. That storm
was unbelievably scary.
XOXO

The world's harshest place:
THE OUTBACK, AUSTRALIA

IT'S TIME TO HEAD DOWN UNDER

You wave goodbye to Venezuela and sail through the Panama Canal. You're going to cross almost nine thousand miles of the Pacific Ocean. You're headed down under to Australia, but first you've got to cross a belt of windless water near the Equator called the doldrums.

After two weeks without so much as a puff of wind in your sails, Ecuador's magical Galapagos Islands come into view—home to giant tortoises! Then it's a mammoth journey, island-hopping through paradise. Finally, the gleaming white sail-like roof of Sydney's Opera House greets you. Welcome to Australia. It's beautiful . . .
BUT IT'S GOT BITE!

Watch out for venomous snakes, and make sure you check under the dunny for lurking spiders!

Australia is a land of extremes. While one part of the country battles drought, another might brace for cyclones. Yet the Aboriginal people, who settled here around 65,000 years ago, found ways to live in harmony with nature. They're one of the world's oldest surviving societies and the traditional owners of the land. Made up of over five hundred clan groups and living from the coasts to the center, they have their own languages and cultures. You'll get a chance to visit and learn from the Anangu clan in the Red Centre—the middle of the Australian Outback. It's remote and ferociously hot there, even in the shade. And it's a five-day train ride away.

The scenery whizzes by as the train rolls on. There's an abundance of kangaroos and cattle stations bigger than some countries. You finally pull into a wall of heat. Your head is suddenly engulfed by what feels like hundreds of flies. One's even daringly perched on your eyelid! Grab your billycan—that's what you'll cook with for the next few days. It's far more practical than the Chinese gong carried by **Robert O'Hara Burke** and **William John Wills** on their attempt to cross Australia south to north in 1860. *BONG!* No point standing around sweating . . .

Let's go.

The world's harshest place:
THE OUTBACK, AUSTRALIA

👃 CAN YOU SMELL THAT?

You're a tourist on the Anangu people's land, and you're going to learn how they make the Outback their home. The air is hot and heavy with dust, and there's a faint, minty tang of crushed eucalyptus leaves on the breeze. Your friend the camel is back—there really is no better teammate. Just ask **Robyn Davidson**, who trekked 1,700 miles across Australia in 1977. It took her nine months to cross two deserts with four camels and her dog, Diggity.

Don't. Move. A. Muscle.

👆 CAN YOU FEEL THAT?

It's hot enough to fry an egg on the ground. While cooling down under a ghost gum tree, something heavy slithers over your boot. You look down at the gleaming, brown-scaled body of a highly venomous mulga snake. Stay very still!

👂 CAN YOU HEAR THAT?

Out here, the endless tick, tick, ticking cicada song soars to 120 decibels—as loud as a rock concert! At sunset, a kookaburra joins the ruckus. **KOO KOO KOO KOO KAA KAA KAAAAA!** Its laughter bounces off the canyon walls as you crawl into your swag, desperate for some peace and quiet.

👅 CAN YOU TASTE THAT?

The sun rises and you wake to yet more birdsong:
the chittering of honeyeaters drifting across the dune.
What's for breakfast today? You reach for a few fat little
honeypot ants—their bellies are as big as grapes. As
each sac pops, sweet syrup explodes in your mouth.
(Afterward, put the live ant back where you found it!)

👁 CAN YOU SEE THAT?

It's been four weeks of plodding through golden grass
and dry, stony creek beds. Just as you're about to give
up, your spirits soar. Solemnly rising from the sand is the
world's largest single-rock monolith: Uluru, also called
Ayers Rock. An ancient rock so red, it's as though it's on
fire. This mountain island (an inselberg) is six hundred
million years old and sacred to the Anangu people.
Every curve, cave, and crevice has a special meaning,
capturing events of creation periods. You're so honored
to experience this sacred place.

Taking in one last deep, sandy breath,
you climb into a solar plane and say
farewell to the Outback.

Next stop will be
BRRilliant.

Dear Mom & Dad,
The camels are dusty, thirsty, and
fly-ridden, and I'm worse! But at
least I survived the Outback!

I miss you.

XOXO

The world's stinkiest place:
ZAVODOVSKI ISLAND

THIS IS NO ORDINARY ISLAND

You knew the next stop was an island, but you forgot what kind. You're on a ship bound for the South Sandwich Islands in the South Atlantic Ocean. They're a chain of volcanic islands surrounded by a raging sea. You're off to Zavodovski—the stinkiest of them all. And in more bad news: black clouds are rolling in. Batten down the hatches! As mountainous waves slam against the ship, you quickly get below deck.

Hunkered down, the crew swaps hair-raising stories of adventurers who've battled the sea. In 2015, **Sarah Outen** was rowing across the Atlantic on a four-year adventure around the globe when a hurricane forced her to abandon her boat, *Happy Socks*. In 2019, **Lee Spencer** rowed solo across the Atlantic. Lee uses a prosthetic leg after losing his right leg in a car accident. It made balancing the unstable boat especially difficult. Yet he beat the record of every person who completed this journey before him.

LAND AHOY!

Strong winds whip the waves into thirty-foot peaks, tossing your ship like a paper boat. Lunch lurches in your stomach. Hold on tight!

After two weeks battling storms, you see craggy, broken, black island cliffs jutting out of the churning sea as though a monster is baring its fangs.

You've reached Zavodovski.

The world's stinkiest place:
ZAVODOVSKI ISLAND

👆 CAN YOU FEEL THAT?

You clamber into an inflatable boat to get closer to shore, and the freezing cold waves chill you to your core. You count down: **3, 2, 1... JUMP!** You claw your way onto the island. You're damp, panting, and shivering, but you're finally on land.

👁 CAN YOU SEE THAT?

Wait! Did something just move? As the mist clears, you discover that more than one million beady-eyed penguins are staring you down. Zavodovski is home to an enormous colony of chinstrap and macaroni penguins. The foaming sea is rich with life, and the penguins dive in to snag their supper.

👃 CAN YOU SMELL THAT?

The island reeks like rotten shrimp in the sun. That's the guano—penguin poop. But there's something even smellier here: Mount Asphyxia, the island's big, angry volcano. You shove a tissue up each nostril and climb into your tent to escape the smell.

But there is no escape!

🦻 CAN YOU HEAR THAT?

SPLAT! The grumpy penguins poo on your tent because you're in the way of the daily flow of penguin traffic. Screeching skuas soar overhead as Antarctic fur seals huff and puff on the shore. Try to sleep, but keep one ear open for volcanic booms. The last thing you want is a giant slug of lava to land on your tent, too.

👅 CAN YOU TASTE THAT?

You've slept in a lightning storm, a jaguar-infested rain forest, and the belly of a cave. But last night was easily your worst sleep. Ever. You kept waking up, gagging from the smell. Now you can taste bitter ash on your lips. Remember: Mount Asphyxia is an active volcano, and it's been hissing all night. Time to get off this island.

Say farewell to your feisty flippered friends. An icebreaker is moored offshore waiting for you. Onward to the bottom of the world!

Dear Mom & Dad,
Captain James Cook described Zavodovski as the most "horrible coast on Earth, doomed by nature never to see the warmth of a sunray." I thought he was being dramatic. Now that I've been pooped on by 314 penguins, I TOTALLY AGREE!
XOXO

The world's coldest place: ANTARCTICA

THE WHITE WILDERNESS IS WAITING

Antarctica is a barren polar desert about the size of the United States and Mexico combined. Fog blankets the Southern Ocean, hiding icebergs that snap and rumble in the dark. Your ship carefully weaves through narrow passages and past giant cathedrals of ice. The searchlight sweeps over the ocean, helping you look out for ice floes too big to tackle. The coldest temperature recorded in Antarctica was a bone-chilling –28.6 degrees Fahrenheit (ten times colder than a bathtub of ice). Because of this, only a small number of plants grow in Antarctica, and it's home to just a few (cold) scientists and animals, including penguins, seals, migrating birds, and whales.

Antarctica has beaten even the most experienced explorers. Legend has it that Irish explorer **Ernest Shackleton** wrote this ad for his 1907 expedition: "Men wanted for hazardous journey. Small wages, bitter cold, long months of complete darkness, constant danger. Safe return doubtful." If only he'd foreseen his ship, *Endurance*, getting crushed in the ice and stranding his twenty-eight-man crew. After two years battling the ice and sea, they all made it out alive.

In 1912, England's **Robert Falcon Scott** was racing Norway's **Roald Amundsen** to the South Pole when Scott's crew got caught in a blizzard, and their supplies ran out. Amundsen won the race, and Scott and many on his team perished.

Your journey across Antarctica is what explorers call an "unsupported" expedition, with everything you need attached to your pulk sled. You'll drag close to 200 pounds of food and supplies across 1,740 miles of ice. You've crammed a few practical things in, too, including sunglasses to cut glare from the ice and lip balm for when the dry air cracks your lips.

At last, your ship docks in the frozen Weddell Sea, which looks like an icy jigsaw puzzle. You take your first frozen steps.

The world's coldest place:
ANTARCTICA

👁 CAN YOU SEE THAT?

You spend weeks hauling your pulk across the ice shelf, which twinkles like frosted glass. Then you travel along the windswept Antarctic plateau. Now here's the sastrugi fields: an obstacle course of frozen waves carved by wind. You recall reading that in 2009 **Mark Pollock** became the first blind person to reach the South Pole. His teammate tugged a ribbon to tell Mark where the sastrugi were, and he still fell about fifty times.

Aahhh!

🔊 CAN YOU HEAR THAT?

The wind roars across the ice as fast as a cheetah. You shuffle one ski in front of the other: **SCRUNCH, SWOOSH.** Then the ice gives way like a trapdoor, leaving you dangling inside a massive crevasse almost fifty feet wide. Luckily, you're anchored by the rope attached to your pulk. Slowly and carefully, you pull yourself up.

👆 CAN YOU FEEL THAT?

After seven weeks of trekking, you gather up your last scrap of energy. Your heart races with excitement as you stretch out your fingertips and finally touch the mirrored ball of the South Pole. You've reached the bottom of the planet!

Do you remember what happened to **Tom Crean** from Scott's expedition? One of his companions collapsed and Crean had to find help. He trekked eighteen hours alone, carrying just a few cookies and some chocolate. He saved that man's life.

👃 CAN YOU SMELL THAT?

You're determined to follow in the brave footsteps of **Børge Ousland**, who in 1996 became the first person to cross Antarctica solo. You spend six exhausting weeks zigzagging downhill to McMurdo Research Station. After smelling nothing but your own putrid socks for so long, it's a relief to catch a fishy whiff of the cute but stinky Weddell seals.

👅 CAN YOU TASTE THAT?

Inside the ramshackle hut that Scott's team erected, the shelves groan under the weight of jars and cans. You fire up an oil lamp and slide into your sleeping bag to get warm. That's when you spot it high on a shelf: Scott's chocolate stash. You open the tin and discover that it's perfect inside. You've earned every hundred-year-old mouthful.

There's one last surprise for you on this expedition.

Are you ready?

Dear Mom & Dad,

Antarctica was COLD, the ice was HARD, and my lips are CRACKED. This next stop better be relaxing.

Love you.

XOXO

The most out-of-this-world place:
MARS

IS THERE LIFE ON MARS?

The final leg of your journey is going to be extremely dangerous, cold, and far away. Suit up! Your next stop? Mars. As well as being one of our closest planetary neighbors, Mars is a lot like Earth, with volcanoes, polar ice caps, and seasons. Many scientists believe there might even be life there, too! After flying on a military plane to the United States, you're whisked away in a limousine to the launchpad. Your stomach flip-flops as you catch the first glimpse of your silver starship. You scramble into your launch suit, ride the lift up the launch tower, and stride to your spaceship. Don't forget to fasten your seatbelt!

Astronauts in position.
Twenty seconds and counting.
T minus 15 seconds.

12, 11, 10, 9 . . .
Ignition sequence start . . .
6, 5, 4, 3, 2, 1, 0 . . .
All engines running.
WE HAVE LIFTOFF!

Everything's shaking as the rocket boosters roar with the power of twenty jumbo jets. The incredible acceleration pins you to your seat as you go **UP, UP, UP.** After nine terrifying minutes . . . you're in space.

Not many people get to travel far from Earth, and no human has been to Mars yet. **SPACE TRAVEL IS DANGEROUS.** Without your suit, you'd boil alive. But the danger is worth it for the view, right?

It's out of this world.

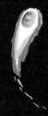

Fewer than thirty people have ever traveled beyond Earth's orbit. How does it feel to make history? But now it's time to rest. You didn't expect to stay awake all the way to Mars, did you? Climb into your space pod and get ready for cryosleep, a kind of hibernation that will keep your body healthy for the next nine months and prevent extreme boredom, called cabin fever. Sleep tight.

WAKE UP! You're preparing to land. The engine fires and everything slows and then . . . touchdown.

Welcome, Earthlings!

The most out-of-this-world place:
MARS

👆 CAN YOU FEEL THAT?

You put on your Extravehicular Mobility Unit (EMU) and explore Mars! This spacesuit weighs more than a giant panda, with fourteen layers to protect you. Inside you'll find oxygen (important), a drink bag (essential), and a diaper (embarrassing). Your earpiece crackles.

"Okay, astronaut, you're clear to come out."

🔊 CAN YOU HEAR THAT?

You bounce onto Mars's red, rocky surface, and your boots stir up dust. The air is a hundred times thinner than on Earth, so sound doesn't travel in the same way. If you took off your helmet and screamed, you'd barely hear a whisper. But please don't—humans can't breathe the air on Mars! Rovers clank past, taking pictures and collecting soil and rocks. That's how scientists discovered that water is trapped underground here.

What other secrets is Mars hiding?

👃 CAN YOU SMELL THAT?

After a few hours bouncing in low gravity, you climb back inside the rocket for a break. That faintly metallic smell is Martian dust. Careful not to get it on your skin—it could burn! You read about it before you got here, but no words quite accurately capture the strange, bitter smell.

👅 CAN YOU TASTE THAT?

All food in space is dehydrated to keep travel weight down. Your little bag of mush is a Sunday roast—you just add water at the rehydration station before you eat it. Tortillas are an astronaut favorite. They don't create crumbs, and you can slather almost anything on them. Some astronauts like to cover their tortillas with applesauce and peanut butter. Do you think that'll catch on back home?

👁 CAN YOU SEE THAT?

After three months exploring Mars, it's time to begin the nine-month journey home. You're desperate for a bath. By the time you land, you'll have had only sponge baths for nearly two years. As you leave the Red Planet behind, you enjoy one last dusky blue sunset. What a strange but beautiful planet.

Your earpiece crackles:

"Command . . . we're heading home."

Dear Mom and Dad,

I feel as small as a speck of dust out here among the stars.

I miss you!

See you soon!

XOXO

MISSION COMPLETE

You've been adventuring for three years, two months, and three weeks. Your hair is halfway down your back. You've got jungle rot on your left foot. And you just realized that a tarantula has been living in your backpack since the first stop on your trip. After all this time, what if your family doesn't recognize you?

But luckily your family is here to greet you. It's the world's most welcome bear hug, with no bear spray required. **You're finally home!**

Later as you stare at your postcards dangling off the fridge, you do the math of your expedition.

COUNTRIES AND TERRITORIES VISITED: 24

PLANETS VISITED: 2

MILES TRAVELED: More than 66,270, plus another 300 million miles to Mars and back

ANIMAL SPECIES SPOTTED: 44

INSECT BITES: 102,456 (still itchy!)

REHYDRATED SPACE MEALS: 1,595

CANNED FOOD AND NOODLE PACKETS: 3,572 (including sardines—never again!)

LOST SOCKS: 11

MODES OF TRANSPORT: 22 (and most were eco-friendly, too!)

CHOCOLATE BARS: 86 (one tasted like nothing, but you made up for it!)

You feel tired. A bit hungry. But mostly . . . **HAPPY** to be home at last.

You're a real sport!
Good luck on the rest of your journey!
We miss you!
So long and GOOD LUCK!

THE AGE OF ADVENTURE

Quick, hide your map. . . . If your parents catch you plotting your next adventure or find that tarantula in your bag, you'll be in BIG trouble. But you hear it: the wild is calling. And you can't resist.

BUT WHERE TO NEXT?

People have circumnavigated Earth countless times. We've been up the highest mountains, along the longest rivers, and used satellites whizzing above our heads to chart the most secret parts. It makes you wonder if there are any blank spots left on the map or great feats still to accomplish.

Then you remember what the captain said before you dived into Challenger Deep: over 80 percent of the ocean is yet to be explored. Imagine what's hiding in its inky depths? Plus there are mountains we've never skied down, peaks we've never summited, parts of the poles where humans have never walked, and nobody has swum across the Pacific Ocean. . . .

. . . And that's before you even start on the other planets. Once you begin thinking like that, the spirit of adventure knows no bounds.

A LIFETIME OF EXPEDITIONS AWAIT

People have also started exploring with less equipment and tougher routes. Italian mountaineer **Reinhold Messner** has climbed all fourteen of the world's tallest peaks without oxygen. **Pablo Signoret**, **Rafael Bridi**, and **Guilherme Coury** set a record when they walked a 656-foot-long slackline between two peaks of the French Alps, 10,000 feet above ground! But that takes YEARS of actual training, so no tightrope walking on the backyard clothesline, please.

Humans are always finding ways to go beyond what has been achieved before, pushing their limits further.

BUT WE NEED TO TAKE CARE OF OUR ONLY HOME

Someday perhaps humans will actually visit Mars. But there's one thing that returning from outer space has made you realize. Right now Earth is the only planet where humans can live, so we need to take care of it. And you don't even need to go far away for an adventure! You can squelch through muddy woods, clamber over rocky shores, and spot creatures snuffling through your neighborhood at night. The more we see of Earth's wonderful places and wild animals, the more we'll learn and the better we can protect it all.

Don't worry about that tarantula in your backpack. Get ready . . .

The world is waiting for you!

where will you go?

GLOSSARY

altitude: The height of something above sea level.

Anangu: A community of Indigenous people in Australia who are the traditional owners of Uluru.

Antarctic plateau: The ice sheet where the South Pole is located.

arepas: Pockets of fried dough with different fillings— a South American delicacy!

billycan: A metal bucket used for boiling water or cooking over an open campfire.

bioluminescence: When a living thing makes its own light.

buttress roots: Wide, above-ground roots that prop up a tree.

carabiners: Metal locking loops used in rock climbing and other activities.

cumulonimbus clouds: Thick, tall clouds that bring storms and rain.

crevasse: A deep crack, often in ice.

cryosleep: When the body's functions pause for the duration of a space journey.

cyclones: Rotating tropical windstorms that form in the South Pacific and Indian Ocean.

death zone: The area on a mountain above 26,250 feet (8,000 meters).

depression: An area of sunken or low land.

dry suit: A special suit that keeps your body warm and dry in cold water.

dunny: An Australian word for toilet.

glacier: A slow-moving river of snow or ice on a mountain or near the North and South Poles.

hadal trench: A deep depression in the sea floor.

icebreaker: A special ship designed to sail through icy waters, breaking up thick ice.

ice floe: A sheet of floating ice.

igloo: A dome-shaped shelter built from blocks of solid snow.

Inuit: Indigenous people who live in what are now Greenland, Canada, and Alaska.

inselberg: A "mountain island"; an isolated hill or mountain.

launch tower: The structure built on a rocket launchpad to help service the rocket and give crew access.

launch suit: The Advanced Crew Escape Suit (ACES), also known as the "pumpkin suit" for its orange color; worn by crew members as they leave Earth.

launchpad: Where a rocket launches from.

lava: Molten or semi-molten rocks on the Earth's surface.

machete: A massive knife.

microbial mats: Carpet-like bacteria sprouting from rocks on the floor of Challenger Deep.

monolith: A single large stone or rock formation.

palafito: A colorful stilt house built over the water in Lake Maracaibo.

paleoanthropologist: A scientist who studies human fossils.

plain: A large flat area of land with few trees.

pulk: A sled without runners pulled by a person or dog.

rehydration station: Used on space stations and spaceships to add water to dehydrated food.

rover: A robot used to explore a place humans can't go (such as another planet).

sastrugi: Wave-like ridges in the snow caused by wind.

seniyya: A Sudanese food tray. Yum!

sit-ski: A sled used by skiers who have no or reduced leg movement.

slackline: Similar to a tightrope; someone walks, runs, or balances along a suspended strip of nylon webbing.

solar plane: An airplane powered by energy created from captured sunlight.

speleologist: A person who studies caves.

sump: A cave pit or hollow filled with water.

swag: A waterproof sleeping bag with a hood, for sleeping on the ground without shelter.

tooq: A traditional Inuit tool like an ice pick, used to make a hole in ice.

tributaries: Rivers or streams flowing into a larger river or lake.

PSSST! Did you spot the stowaway throughout the book? That's Herbert, a sneaky tarantula. He climbed into your backpack in the Danakil Depression and traveled all the way around the world with you. See if you can spot him in every place you visited. (He's hiding in twelve locations!)